WHO WOULD WIN?®

GREEN ANTS

VS.

ARMY ANTS

BY
JERRY PALLOTTA
ILLUSTRATED BY
ROB BOLSTER

Scholastic Inc.

The publisher would like to thank the following for their kind permission to use their photographs in this book: Photos ©: 5 center right: Cornel Constantin / Shutterstock; 8 center: B.G. Thomson / Science Source; 17 bee: Nagy Lehel / Shutterstock; 17 fly: annop youngrot / Shutterstock; 17 grasshopper: Geraldas Galinauskas / Shutterstock; 17 scorpion: bonzami emmanuelle / Alamy Stock Photo; 17 mosquito: KPL / Shutterstock; 17 butterfly: Advertising Photography / Alamy Stock Photo; 20 center: Genevieve Vallee / Alamy Stock Photo; 21 top: Dr Morley Read / Science Source; 21 bottom: Mehmet Karatay / Wikipedia; 22 top: Natursports / Shutterstock; 23 top: Henri Koskinen / Alamy Stock Photo.

Welcome to Earth, Lucian Smith Robinson!
— J.P.

To Ant Barbara, Ant Elaine, Ant Pattie, Ant Peg, Ant Sue, and Ant Val.
— R.B.

ISBN: 978-1-338-32024-4

14 13 12   21 22 23 24

Printed in the U.S.A.   40
First printing, 2019

What would happen if green ants had a war against army ants? Who do you think would win?

MEET A GREEN ANT

Scientific name: *Oecophylla smaragdina*. Ants are insects that have a three-section body: head, thorax, and abdomen. The legs of an ant come out of its thorax. Insects have six legs.

abdomen

thorax

head

BODY FACT
Ants have a thin waist.

WIDE-AWAKE FACT
Ants never sleep.

DID YOU KNOW?
Green ants are also called weaver ants or green tree ants.

Green ants live in **Australia**.

World Map

MEET AN ARMY ANT

Scientific name: *Eciton burchelli.* In Africa, army ants are also called *marabunta.*

abdomen

head

thorax

OUCH FACT
An army ant has a stinger at the end of its abdomen.

Most ants and other insects have compound eyes. Army ants have two eyes and are mostly blind.

DEFINITION
A compound eye has hundreds of tiny individual eyes in one.

compound eye close-up

Most army ants live in **South America** and **Africa**.

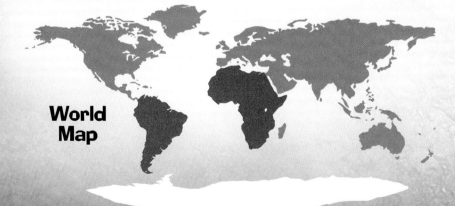

World Map

COLONY

Most green ants live in colonies of about a half million ants.

DEFINITION

An ant colony is a group of ants living and working together.

MATH FACT

A half million equals 500,000 ants.

FACT

A colony could be as few as 20 ants or up to many thousands of ants.

Army ants live in a legion of between a half million and a million individual ants.

Ants have been on Earth for more than 100 million years. Ants were around when dinosaurs walked on Earth. Some ants may have had fights with dinosaurs.

TREES

Green ants live in trees. Why live on the ground when you can live more safely in a tree?

DOWN-TO-EARTH FACT
Except for green ants, almost all other ant species live on the ground.

DID YOU KNOW?
Every ant has a job—some ants cut, other ants hold, and other ants glue.

Green ants weave homes made of leaves. One of the largest green-ant colonies ever seen was spread over 12 trees. Green ants usually stay in one place.

ANT LARVAE

FUN FACT
Green ants use the fluid from their larvae as glue.

DEFINITION
A larva is a young insect.

GROUND

Army ants live on the ground. They do not build permanent places to live. Army ants are often on the move. About every two weeks, they bivouac to another location.

DID YOU KNOW?
A bivouac is a temporary camp.

12 weeks ago

10 weeks ago

8 weeks ago

6 weeks ago

4 weeks ago

FACT
Army ants are nomads.

now

2 weeks ago

MOVEMENT FACT
When ants move, they march in a fan-shaped swarm.

DEFINITION
A nomad lives in more than one place.

DIFFERENT ANTS

There are more than 10,000 different types of ants. We could have matched up many other kinds in this book.

TURTLE ANT

DINOSAUR ANT

LEAF-CUTTER ANT

THIEF ANT

TRAP-JAW ANT

HEARING FACT
Ants do not have ears. They hear through their feet, which pick up vibrations.

BREATHING FACT
Ants do not have lungs. They get oxygen from holes in their bodies called spiracles.

ANT SPIRACLE

extreme close-up

MORE ANTS

Ants are tiny, but they come in all shapes and sizes.

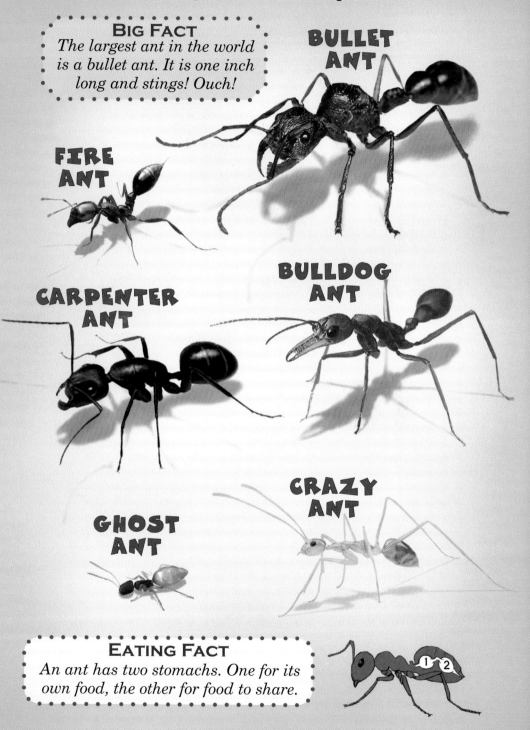

BIG FACT
The largest ant in the world is a bullet ant. It is one inch long and stings! Ouch!

BULLET ANT

FIRE ANT

CARPENTER ANT

BULLDOG ANT

GHOST ANT

CRAZY ANT

EATING FACT
An ant has two stomachs. One for its own food, the other for food to share.

1 2

SOCIETY

Every ant in the green-ant colony has a job to do. Their slogan might be: *Do your job!* Every green ant is like an engineer ready to build a nest or help its colony.

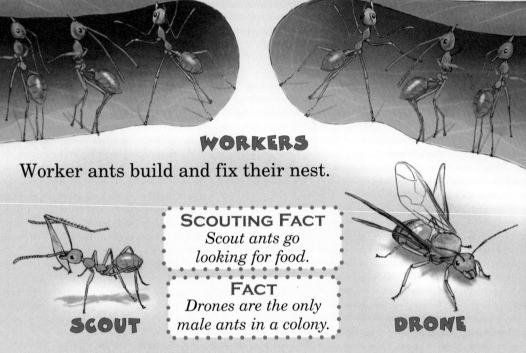

WORKERS

Worker ants build and fix their nest.

SCOUTING FACT
Scout ants go looking for food.

FACT
Drones are the only male ants in a colony.

SCOUT

DRONE

There is only one queen in most ant colonies. The queen lays all the eggs. The colony must protect the queen. If the queen dies, the colony will eventually disappear.

QUEEN

SOLDIER

Soldier ants protect the nest. They fight enemy ants.

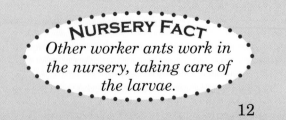

NURSERY FACT
Other worker ants work in the nursery, taking care of the larvae.

FAMILY STRUCTURE

A common human family has a mom, a dad, and a few kids. The average army-ant family has 1 mom (the queen), 20 dads (winged drones), 20 potential new moms (winged princesses), and 500,000–1,000,000 kids (worker ants and soldier ants).

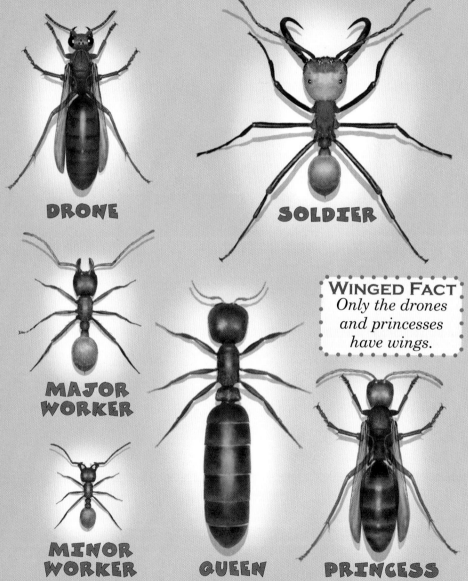

DRONE

SOLDIER

MAJOR WORKER

WINGED FACT
Only the drones and princesses have wings.

MINOR WORKER

QUEEN

PRINCESS

An ant colony has no president, prime minister, or king. But there is a queen. An ant colony thinks together as one unit.

An ant's major weapon is its mandibles.

DEFINITION
*Mandibles are part of
an animal's jaw.*

MANDIBLES

These are the mandibles of a green ant. The mandibles
have moving parts that can bite, pick up, and hold food.

JAWS

The pincers of ants are also called its jaws. This is the jaw of a soldier army ant.

FACT
Many insects live only two weeks.

AGE FACT
Ants are among the longest living of all insects.

DID YOU KNOW?
Some queen ants have lived up to 30 years.

If you were an ant, which jaw would you rather have?

BITE

There are several types of ant jaws.

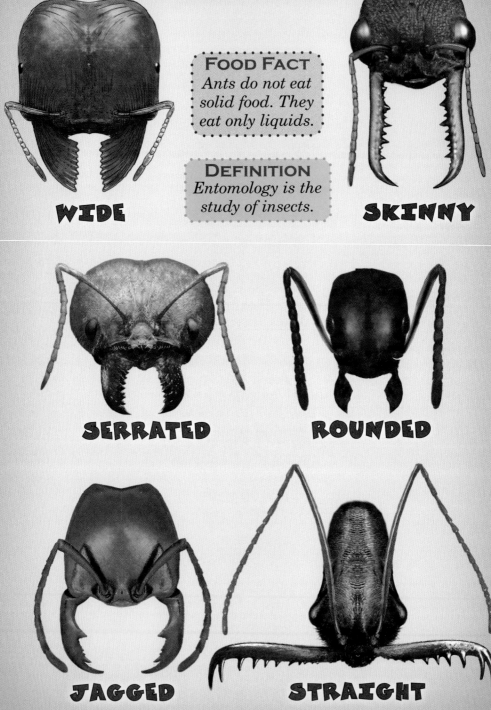

FOOD FACT
Ants do not eat solid food. They eat only liquids.

DEFINITION
Entomology is the study of insects.

WIDE

SKINNY

SERRATED

ROUNDED

JAGGED

STRAIGHT

SIP, CHEW

You can often tell how a bug eats or behaves by its mouth parts.

A **BEE** is a licker. It would enjoy an ice-cream cone just like you might.

A **FLY** is a sponger. When it lands, it "sponges" back and forth looking for food.

A **GRASSHOPPER** is a chewer. Its mouth is shaped to chew grass and leaves.

A **SCORPION** is a pincher. It has no teeth. Its mouth has pincers inside.

A **MOSQUITO** is a bloodsucker. It stabs with its needle-shaped face.

A **BUTTERFLY** is a sipper. It uses its curly tube-shaped proboscis like a straw.

Is a **DARWIN BEETLE** a clipper? No! It uses its long jaws to flip and throw other insects.

STRONG

Ants can lift things that are much heavier than they are. They can raise between 20 and 50 times their own weights.

SPEED FACT
Most ants travel less than 1 mile per hour.

SPEED FACT
Green ants walk a little slower than army ants.

If you were an ant, you could lift . . .

 a car,

DEFINITION
Myrmecology is the scientific study of ants.

 or a pickup truck,

 or maybe an elephant.

Here is a leaf-cutter ant raising a huge chunk of a leaf.

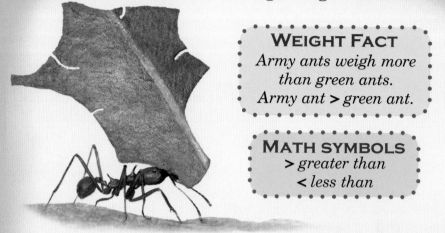

WEIGHT FACT
*Army ants weigh more
than green ants.
Army ant > green ant.*

MATH SYMBOLS
*> greater than
< less than*

This is a dinosaur ant picking up a stone.

Here is a bulldog ant lifting its precious larvae.

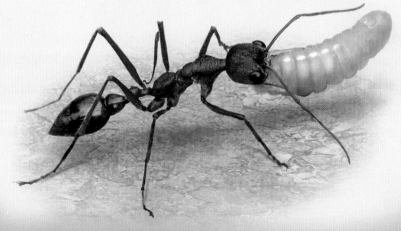

GREATEST WEAPON

The green ants' greatest weapon is their numbers. The ants warn one another of danger by releasing a chemical called a pheromone.

Thousands of ants are called to battle to protect their colony. Ants bite their enemies to death.

Another important weapon is how well organized green ants are. They work together to build an ant bridge across a gap.

GO GREEN
Green ants are camouflaged. They hide more easily in green leaves.

WEAPON

The army ants' greatest weapon is also their huge numbers. Any animal can fight against one ant. But can you fight a million ants?

GROUNDED FACT

Army ants are also camouflaged. They are brown and black. Army ants blend in against the dark ground and dead leaves they walk on.

DEFINITION
Zoology is the study of animals.

"FARMER" ANTS

Leaf-cutter ants are like farmers. They grow their own food. These ants make piles of insect and leaf parts and grow fungus. They eat the fungus.

"STORAGE" ANTS

Honeypot ants store honey in their abdomens so the colony will have food.

FACT
Ants are so organized that scientists use them as models of human behavior.

"COWBOY" ANTS

Herder ants "herd cattle." They capture aphids, a small insect, and corral, or keep them for future meals. The ants eat a liquid produced by the aphids.

"LANDSCAPER" ANTS

Some ants are landscapers. They prune and weed around their colony. Any paths that enemies could use to attack the colony are cut back.

WORD GAME!

Can you solve these word puzzles? Each answer uses **ANT** and a few other letters. We've filled in a few letters—and the first answer—to get you started!

KEY 🐜 = **ANT**

P🐜 S = (pants)

(antler) = 🐜 _ _ _ R

H _ _ _ _ 🐜 = (hydrant)

(elephant) = _ _ _ _ _ 🐜 🐜

L 🐜 _ _ _ _ = (lantern)

Find the answers on page 32.

At the trunk of a tree, a few army ants attack some wandering green ants. The green ants spray folic acid into the air.

The folic acid alerts other green ants nearby to join the fight. They drop what they are doing and head to battle. The spray irritates the army ants' eyes and makes it hard for them to breathe.

Uh-oh! It's a full battle. Thousands of green ants are fighting thousands of army ants.

The green ants try to trick the army ants. The green ants are clever. They divert the fight away from their queen. If she is saved, the colony can live on.

The army ants have greater numbers and start winning the battle.

The army ants advance in an overwhelming force.
Ants, ants, and more army ants.

The green ants retreat. They realize they can't win the massive battle they began. The war is no fun.

The army ants win! There are many dead green ants to eat. The army ants have a feast. The surviving green ants return to their queen. Tomorrow they will rebuild their colony.

WHO HAS THE ADVANTAGE? CHECKLIST

GREEN ANTS		ARMY ANTS
☐	JAWS	☐
☐	ACID SPRAY	☐
☐	STINGER	☐
☐	NUMBERS	☐
☐	SPEED	☐
☐	WEIGHT	☐
☐	CAMOUFLAGE	☐

If you were the author, how would you rewrite the ending?

Puzzle answers: pants, antler, hydrant, elephant, lantern, mantis, antelope, antenna, Antarctica, eggplant